THE PROPHESIES OF NOSTRADAMUS

THE
PROPHESIES
OF
NOSTRADAMUS

※

INCLUDING THE
"PREFACE TO MY SON"
AND THE
"EPISTLE TO HENRY II"

Illustrated by SHARI DE MISKEY

AVENEL BOOKS
NEW YORK

This edition is published by Avenel Books,
distributed by Crown Publishers, Inc.

1980 EDITION

Manufactured in the United States of America

Library of Congress Cataloging in Publication Data

Notredame, Michel de. 1503-1566.
    The prophesies of Nostradamus.

    1. Prophecies (Occult sciences) I. Title.
BF1815.N8A3   1979   133.3   79-24358
ISBN 0-517-30984-X
n   m   l   k   j   i   h   g

BF
1815
.N8
A3
1980

NOSTRADAMUS

[1503–1566]

Michel de Nostredame, born in Provence, in the town of St. Remy, in the year 1503, was the greatest of all prophets of the era of the Renaissance. The general report is that he was of Jewish descent, but of a family that had been converted to Christianity. He is said to have claimed to be of the tribe of Issachar, deriving from this his gift of prophecy, for they were "men that had understanding of the times, to know what Israel ought to do" (I Chron. xii. 32); or, as in Esther i. 13, "the seven wise men that knew the times." This claim has been called into question, as Issachar happens to be one of the ten lost tribes. As we have already seen, however, a whole immense cult today claims descent from the lost tribes, even complete identity with them.

Nostradamus's father was a notary. His mother's ancestors on both her father's and her mother's side were men skilled in mathematics and medicine, a fact which lends credence to their being Jews, for from time immemorial, Jews together with their Semitic brothers the Arabs had retained a proficiency in both sciences. Add to this the fact that Nostradamus had a rather remarkable grandfather who, for a pastime, gave him a taste for the celestial sciences. On the death of this kinsman, Nostradamus went to school at Avignon, where he took humanity courses. Then, at the university of Montpelier, the most famous school of medicine in all France, he studied philosophy and the theory of medicine.

For all its reputation as a medical center, Montpelier could not escape visitation by the plague (probably in 1525), whereupon Nostradamus continued his studies in Narbonne, Toulouse and Bordeaux. He returned to Montpelier for his Doctor's degree, which he won expeditiously and with great *éclat*. He practiced at Toulouse, later at Agen, where he married. His two children died young; his wife also died. He retired to Provence. The Parliament of Provence invited him to Aix. Here he stayed three years, attending on victims of the plague which broke out in 1546 and raged fiercely and for a long period. The town voted him a pension for many years to come for the valuable services he rendered during the contagion.

From Aix he went to Salon de Craux, which lies midway between Avignon and Marseilles. Here he married again, and had three sons and a daughter. It was here, we are told,[1] "that, foreseeing great mutations were about to affect all Europe, and that civil wars and trou-

[1] *Oracles of Nostradamus,* by Charles A. Ward. Chas. Scribner's Sons, 1940.

bles were soon to come upon the kingdom of France, he felt an unaccountable and new enthusiasm springing up uncontrollably in his mind, which at last amounted almost to a maddening fever, till he sat down to write his 'Centuries' and other 'Presages.' "

These prophecies consisted of quatrains composed in an enigmatical mood, resembling more the objective Greek oracles rather than the prognostications of the Hebrew prophets, whose prophetic note was only secondary to the moral fervor with which they were endowed. For a long time he forebore publishing them, fearing as he did their effect on potential detractors and backbiters. In the end, yielding to the temptation of being useful to the public, he published them; though, to be sure, as the commentator points out, their usefulness was of dubious value, since "they could not possibly be understood till they were interpreted after the event and by it."

It appears that he was invited to Lyons in 1547 but soon returned to Salon only to find that his vogue was on the wane. Whereupon, he retired more and more into solitude, developing his powers of divination which he confesses to having practiced for some years. He is said to have arrived at the judgment that a perfect knowledge of medicine required the aid of astrology, which henceforth found in him a devoted student. His first venture in publication was a series of almanacs which enjoyed so huge a vogue in those days. In these he foretold the shape of the things to come with such convincing aptness as to win instant favor. Yet at the same time his worst fears were realized. His work provoked the attack of a section of the public which pronounced him an impostor and a charlatan, while the more moderate critics dubbed him a simple visionary, or, still worse, a fool. On the other hand, he gained the applause of the *élite,* including Henry II and Catherine de Medici.

It is contended that Nostradamus having reached the age of fifty-two when he published his first book, he couldn't possibly have begun a course of imposture at so mature an age. For it is certain that hitherto he had enjoyed the esteem of honest men, had shown proficiency in his chosen profession, had lived an exemplary life and exhibited religious sentiments of a high order.

He first came to the notice of Queen Catherine de Medici and Henry II by the publication, in March, 1555, of the first seven "Centuries" of his "Prophecies." In the following year he was invited to attend the Court in Paris, where he was shown high favor by the King. Though what he told them is not known, it may be assumed that he did not tell them what he knew—that is, in any precise sense; for he couched his prophecies in an enigmatic manner. For the princes, whose tragical fates he correctly set out, were none other than Francis II, Charles IX and Henry III.

He returned to Salon, where he completed his *Centuries,* consisting of three hundred more quatrains, published in 1558. Henry II was killed the following year, at the tournament of St. Quentin, as fully set forth at Quatrain 35 in Century I.

> Le lyon jeune le vieux surmontera
> En champ bellique par singulier duelle:
> Dans cage d'or le yeux lui crevera,
> Deux classes une, puis mourir, mort cruelle.

Translation

The young lion shall overcome the old
On the field of war in a single combat [duelle];
He will pierce his eyes in a cage of gold.
This is the first of two lappings, then he dies a cruel death.

A Court favorite, he received visits at Salon from the royalty; while Charles IX, as he proceeded in 1564 through the country to quell the revolt in the cities, asked first of all for Nostradamus, when he arrived at Salon. He made him Physician in Ordinary and honored him with the title of Counsellor. He complained rather bitterly, however, of the neglect he suffered from his own townsmen, even while the scholars and the grandees of the world were flocking to him to listen to his wisdom, the wisdom of an oracle. A contemporary wrote of him that "those who came to France sought Nostradamus as the only thing to be seen there."

After the visit of King Charles IX he had but a year and four months to live, for he was suffering from severe attacks of gout and other ailments. He foretold the time, even to the day and the hour, of his death. He died on July 2, 1566, at dawn, with all his senses about him. His widow erected to him a marble tablet, with a Latin inscription, the translation of which reads as follows:

Here lie the bones of the illustrious Michael Nostradamus, whose almost divine pen alone, in the judgment of all mortals, was worthy to record, under the influx of stars, the future events of the whole world. He lived 62 years, 6 months, 17 days. He died at Salon in the year 1566. Posterity, disturb not his sweet rest! Anne Ponce Gemelle hopes for her husband true felicity.

By this wife, his second, Nostradamus had three sons and three daughters. It was to Cæsar, the eldest, that he dedicated the first seven of the "Centuries," a Dedication herewith reproduced in full, since it reveals the workings of a mind which must interest all who are intrigued by the peculiar skill that makes prophets.

PRÉFACE À MON FILS

The Preface of Michael Nostradamus to His Prophecies

To Cæsar Nostradamus his son, life and felicity. Thy late arrival,[3] Cæsar Nostradamus my son, has made me bestow much time, through nightly vigils, to leave you in writing a

---

[3] Cæsar Nostradamus was born at the beginning of 1555, so he was but a few weeks old when his father dedicated to him the first four "Centuries," published for the first time in 1555, by Macé Bonhomme, the printer at Lyons. In the name of this son the epistle is really a dedication to his spiritual sons; that is, to his interpreters and students in all future ages.

memorial to refer to, after the corporal extinction of your
progenitor, that might serve for the common profit of mankind, out of what the Divine Being has permitted me to learn
from the revolution of the stars. And since it has pleased the
immortal God that thou shouldst come into the natural light
of this terrene abode, and shouldst say that thy years are not
yet calculated astronomically, and thy March months are in-
capable to receive in their weak understanding what I must
necessarily record [as to happen] after my time:—seeing also
that it is not possible to leave thee in writing what might suffer
injury and be obliterated by time; for the inherited gift of
occult prediction will remain confined to my own bowels:—
considering that events of human proposal are uncertain, whilst
all is governed and directed by the incalculable power of
Heaven, guiding us, not by Bacchic fury, nor yet by Lym-
pathic[4] motion, but by astronomical assertion—"*Soli numine
divino afflati præsagiunt et spirito prophetico particularia.*"[5]

Although for years past I have predicted, a long time in

[4]Lymphatics, Garencières (p. 16) tells, were anciently those who
were mad for love; and he absurdly adds that the sign of it was, that
such persons threw themselves into the water,—*lympha* maning water. Varro says that in Greece those who were mad were called
νυμφολήπτους which means caught by nymphs. Festus, to fit this,
thinks that men went mad by seeing the image of nymphs in the
water fountains. Others have it that they were afraid of water, as if
it were hydrophobia that possessed them. But *nympha* and *lympha*
approach each other so nearly, that when a man is once caught by
a nymph he is, for the time being, mad to all intents and purposes,
—"it is not given to a man to love and to be wise." Leaving all this
to be settled as it may, there is no question but in the medical
technology of Nostradamus a deep melancholy is what was understood by the Lymphatic motion,—melancholy being the temperament
most apt for study, poetry, and vaticination. Garencières invents a
word for the occasion, or uses one that has since grown obsolete. He
employs the verb *lymphatize.*

[5]"Such alone as are inspired by the divine power can predict particular events in a spirit of prophecy."

advance, what has afterwards come to pass, and in particular regions attributing the whole accomplishment to divine power and inspiration, also other unfortunate and fortunate occurrences have been pronounced with accelerated promptitude which have since happened in other parts of the world—for I was willing to maintain silence and to pass over matters that might prove injurious [if published] not only as relates to the present time, but also for the most part of future time, if committed to writing, since kingdoms, sects, and religions will pass through stages so very contrary, and, as regards the present time, diametrically opposed—that if I were to relate what will happen in the future, governors, sectaries, and ecclesiastics would find it so ill-accordant with [*si*] their auricular fancy, that they would go near to condemn what future ages will know and perceive to be true. Considering also the sentence of the true Saviour, "*Nolite sanctum dare canibus neque mittatis margaritas vestras ante porcos, ne forte conculcent eas pedibus suis, et conversi dirumpant vos*" [Matt. vii. 6].

This it is which has led me to withhold my tongue from the vulgar, and my pen from paper. But, later on, I thought I would enlarge a little, and declare in dark and abstruse sayings in consideration of [*pour*] the vulgar advent [vid. Le Pelletier, i. 163] the most urgent of its future causes, as perceived by me, be the revolutionary changes what they may, so only as not to scandalize the auricular frigidity (of my hearers), and write all down under a cloudy figure that shall essentially and above all things be prophetical. Although "*Abscondidisti hæc à sapientibus, et prudentibus, id est, potentibus, et regibus, et enucleasti ea exiguis et tenuibus.*"[6] By the grace of God and the good angels, the Prophets have

[6]"Thou hast hidden these things from the wise and prudent, *i.e.,* from the powerful and from kings, and hast revealed them to the small and weak." This is Nostradamus's gloss upon Matt. xi. 25.

had committed to them the spirit of vaticination, by which they see things at a distance, and are enabled to forecast future events. For there is nothing that can be accomplished without Him, whose power and goodness are so great to all His creatures as long as they put their trust in Him, much as they may be [exposed] or subject to other influences, [yet] on account of their likeness to the nature of their good guardian angel [or genius] that heat and prophetic power draweth nigh to us, as do the rays of the sun which cast their influence alike upon bodies that are elementary and non-elementary. As for ourselves personally who are but human, we can attain to nothing by our own unaided natural knowledge, nor the bent of our intelligence, in the way of deciphering the recondite secrets of God the Creator. *"Quia non est nostrum noscere tempora, nec momenta,"*[7] etc. Although, indeed, now or hereafter some persons may arrive to whom God Almighty may be pleased to reveal by imaginative impression some secrets of the future, as accorded in time past to judicial astrology, when [*que* for *quand*] a certain power and volitional faculty came upon them, as a flame of fire appears.[8] They grew inspired, and were able to judge of all inspiration, human and divine, alike. For the divine works, which are absolutely universal, God will complete; those which are contingent, or medial, the good

---

[7]Acts i. 7.

[8]Nostradamus seems, whenever he alludes to this appearance of flame as preceding vaticination, to have in his mind the descent of tongues of fire at Pentecost (Acts ii. 3), διαμεριζόμεναι γλῶσσαι ὡσεὶ πυρός. A flame of fire, be it observed, conveys a double symbol: it resembles a tongue in form. Its luminousness and its purifying tendency express the celestial nature of spirit, as contrasted with matter, and also inspiration. So that intrinsically and extrinsically it represents prophetic utterance. Grotius contributes an unusually good note upon this passage, pointing out that as in Genesis (xi. 9), confusion of tongues scattered mankind, so here (Acts ii. 3) the gift of tongues was to bring men again into one brotherhood.

angels direct; and the third sort come under the evil angels.[9]

Perhaps, my son, I speak to thee here a little too occultly. But as to the hidden vaticinations which come to one by the subtle spirit of fire, or sometimes by the understanding disturbed, [it may even be, by] contemplating the remotest stars, as being intelligences on the watch, even to giving utterance to declarations [that] being taken down in writing declare, without favour, and without any taint of improper loquacity, that all things whatsoever proceed from the divine power of the great eternal Deity from whom all goodness emanates. Further, my son, although I have inserted the name of prophet, I do not desire to assume a title of so high sublimity at the present moment. For he who *"Propheta dicitur hodie, olim vocabatur videns"*;[10] for, strictly speaking, my son, a prophet is one who sees things remote from the knowledge of all mankind. Or, to put the case; to the prophet, by means of the perfect light of prophecy, there lie opened up very manifestly divine things as well as human; which cannot come about, seeing that the effects of future prediction extend to such remote periods. Now, the secrets of God are incomprehensible, and their efficient virtue belongs to a sphere far remote from natural knowledge; for, deriving their immediate origin from the free will, things set in motion causes that of themselves could never attract such attention as could make them recognized, either by human augury, or by any other knowledge of occult power;

[9]This passage is very difficult to bring to a clear sense in translation. Garencières has simply evaded it. It seems to mean that God operates all the great effects in the universe; that, as He is the Maker, so is He the perpetual operator in the world,—its cause and life; but that the guardian angels are good and bad, and are charged with some sort of duty and office, not as affecting the mechanic frame of the world, but in respect of mankind. This is in conformity with the Cabala and Hermetical teaching; but what he precisely means cannot, I think, be quite absolutely stated.

[10]"He who is called prophet now, once was called seer."

it is a thing comprised only within the concavity of heaven itself, from the present fact of all eternity, which comes in itself to embrace all time.

Still, by the means of some eternal power, by an epileptic Herculean agitation, the causes by the celestial movement became known. I do not say, my son, in order that you may fully understand me, that the knowledge of this matter cannot yet impress itself upon thy feeble brain, that very remote future causes may not come within the cognizance of a reasonable being; if they are, notwithstanding, purely the creation of the intellectual soul of things present, future things are not by any means too hidden or concealed. But the perfect knowledge of causes cannot be acquired without divine. inspiration; since all prophetic inspiration derives its first motive principle from God the Creator, next from good fortune, and then from nature. Wherefore the independent causes being independently produced, or not produced, the presage partially happens, where it was predicted. For the human understanding, being intellectually created, cannot˙ penetrate occult causes, otherwise than by the voice of a genius by means of the thin flame (*vid.* page 76) [showing] to what direction future causes incline to develop themselves. And further, my son, I implore you never to apply your understanding on such reveries and vanities as dry up the body and bring perdition.to the soul and disturb all the senses. In like manner, I caution you against the seduction of a more than execrable magic, that has been denounced already by the sacred Scriptures, by the divine canons of the Church—although we have to exempt from this judgment Judicial Astrology. By the aid of this it is, and by divine revelation and inspiration, united with deep calculations, we have reduced our prophecies to writing. And, notwithstanding that this occult philosophy was *not* reproved by the Church, I have felt no desire to divulge their unbridled promptings. Although many volumes have come before me, which had laid hidden for many ages. But dreading what might happen in the future, after reading them, I presented them to Vulcan, and as the fire kindled them, the flame, licking the air, shot forth an unaccustomed brightness, clearer than the light is of natural flame, resembling more the explosion of powder, casting a subtle illumination over the house as if the whole were wrapped in sudden conflagration.—So that at last you might not in the future be abused by searching for the perfect transformation, lunar or solar, or incorruptible metals hidden under the earth, or the sea, I reduced them to ashes.— But as to the judgment which perfects itself by means of the celestial judgment, that I am desirous to manifest to you: by that method you may have cognizance of things future, avoiding all fantastic imaginations that may arise, and limiting the particularity of the topics by divine and supernatural inspiration; harmonizing with the celestial figures these topics, and that part of time, which the occult property has relation to, by the potential virtue and faculty divine, in whose presence the three aspects of time are clasped in one by eternity—an evolution that connects in one causes past, present, and future— "quia omnia sunt nuda et aperta, etc."[11]

From all which, my son, you can easily comprehend, notwithstanding your tender brain, the things that are to happen can be foretold by nocturnal and celestial lights, which are natural, coupled to a spirit of prophecy—not that I would assume the name or efficacy of a prophet, but, by revealed inspiration, as a mortal man the senses place me no farther from heaven than the feet are from the earth. "Possum non errare, falli, decipi,"[12] (albeit) I am the greatest sinner in this world, and heir to every human affliction. But being surprised some-

---

[11]"For all things are naked and open."
[12]"I am able not to err, fail, or be deceived."

times in the ecstatic work, amid prolonged calculation, and
engaged in nocturnal studies of sweet odour, I have composed
books of prophecies, containing each one hundred astronomic
quatrains of forecasts, which I have tried to polish through
obscurely, and which are perpetual vaticinations, from now to
the year 3797. It is possible that this figure will make some lift
up their forehead, at such a vast extent of time, and variety of
things to take place under the concave journey of the moon;
and this universal treatment of causes, my son, throughout the
earth, which, if you reach the natural age of man, you will
see in your climate, under the heaven of your proper nativity,
as things that have been foreseen.

Although the everlasting God alone knows the eternity of
the light proceeding from Himself, I say frankly to all to
whom He has decreed in long and melancholy inspiration to
reveal His limitless magnitude, which is beyond both mensura-
tion and comprehension, that by means of this occult cause
divinely manifested, principally by two chief causes, comprised
in the understanding of the inspired one who prophesies. One
is that which comes by infusion, which clarifies the supernatural light, in him who predicts by astral process, or forecasts by
inspired revelation, which is practically a participation in the
divine eternity, by which means the prophet comes to judge
of that which his share of divine spirit has given him, by means
of communication with God the Creator, and the natural
endowment accorded him. It is to know that what is predicted
is true, and has had a heavenly origin; that such light and the
thin flame is altogether efficacious; that it descends from
above, no less than does natural clearness; and natural light
renders philosophers quite sure of their principles, so that by
means of the principles of a first cause they have penetrated
the profoundest abysses and attained the loftiest doctrines.

But to this end, my son, that I may not wander too pro-

foundly for the future capacity of thy senses, and also because
I find that letters shall suffer great and incomparable loss, and
that I find the world before the universal conflagration, such
deluges and deep submersion, that there will remain scarcely
any land not covered with water, and that for so long a period,
that everything will perish except Ethnographies and Topog-
raphies. Further, after and before these inundations, in many
districts the rains will have been so slight, and there will fall
from heaven such an abundance of fire and incandescent
stones, that scarcely anything will remain unconsumed, and
this will occur a short time before the last conflagration. Further, when the planet Mars completes its cycle, at the end of
this second period, he will recommence his course. But some
will gather in Aquarius through several years, and others in
Cancer, which will be of still longer duration. Now that we
are conducted by the moon, under the direction of the Creator,
and before she has finished her entire circuit the sun will come,
and then Saturn. Now, according to the celestial signs, the
reign of Saturn shall come back again, so that, all calculated,
the world is drawing on towards its anaragonic revolution.

From the time I am writing this, before 177 years 3 months
and 11 days, by pestilence, long famine, and wars, and more
still by inundations, the world between this day and that, before and after, shall be diminished, and its population so reduced that there will hardly be hands enough to attend to
agriculture, and the lands will be left as long without culture
as they have been under tillage. This, so far as celestial judgment manifests, that we are now in the seventh millenary,
which completes all and introduces us to the eighth, where
is the upper firmament of the eighth sphere, which, in a lati-
tudinary dimension, is where the Almighty will come to complete the revolution, where the celestial figures will return to
their courses, and the upper motion which renders the earth

stable for us and fixed, *"non inclinabitur in seculum seculorum,"*[13] unless His will be accomplished, and no otherwise.

Although by ambiguous opinions exceeding all natural reason by Mahometical dreams, also sometimes God the Creator by the ministry of angels of fire, and missive flame, presents to the external senses, even of our eyes, the causes of future predictions, that indicate the future event which must manifest itself to him who presages anything. For the presage which is made by the exterior light comes infallibly to judge partly with and by means of the exterior flame; although truly the part which seems to come by the eye of the understanding springs only from the lesion of the imaginative sense. The reason is too evident, the whole is predicted by the afflatus of divinity, and by means of the angelic spirit inspired to the man prophesying, rendering him [as it were] anointed with vaticinations, visiting him to illuminate him, and, stirring the forefront of his phantasy by divers nightly apparitions no less than daily certitude, he prophesies by astronomic administration conjoined with the holiest future prediction, taking nothing into his consideration but the hardihood of his free courage.

Come at this hour to understand, my son, that I find by my revelations [astral], and which are in accordance with revealed inspiration, that the sword of death is on its way to us now, in the shape of pestilence, war (more horrible than has been known for three generations of men), and famine, that shall fall upon the earth, and return upon it at frequent intervals. For the stars accord with such a revolution, and with the written word, *"Visitabo in virgâ ferrea iniquitates eorum, et in verberibus percutiam eos."*[14] For the mercy of God, my son,

[13]"Whence it shall not deviate from age to age."

[14]"I will visit their iniquities with a rod of iron, and with blows will strike them." This somewhat resembles a passage in the Psalms (ii. 7), but it is not a quotation.

will not be spread abroad for a time, till the major part of my
prophecies shall have been accomplished, and have become
by accomplishment resolved. Thus oftentimes in the course of
these sinister storms the Lord will say, *"Conteram ego, et con-
fringam, et non miserebor."*[15] And a thousand other accidents
will come by waters and continual rain, as I have more fully
and at large set forth in my other Prophecies, which are drawn
out at length, *in solutâ oratione;*[16] (in these I) designate the
localities, times, and terms prefixed, that all men who come
after may see, recognizing the circumstances that come about
by infallible indications. As we have marked by the others
where we speak more clearly, for although they are covered
with a veil of cloud, they are clear enough to be comprehended
by men of good intelligence: *"Sed quando submoventa erit
ignorantia,"*[17] the total will stand out with greater clearance
still. Making an end here, my son, take now this gift of thy
father, Michael Nostradamus, hoping to expound to thee each
several prophecy of these quatrains here given, beseeching the
immortal Father that He will endue thee with a long life of
happy and prospering felicity.

From Salon, this 1st of March, 1555.

Epistle to Henry II

To the most invincible, very puissant, and most Christian
Henry King of France the Second: Michael Nostradamus, his
most humble, most obedient servant and subject, wishes victory
and happiness.

[15]"I will trample them and break them, and not show pity." This
resembles Isai. lxiii. 3.
[16]In prose, and not in verse, as the quatrains are. These prose
forecastings have, I am afraid, been altogether lost.
[17]"When the time arrives for the removal of ignorance."

For that sovereign observation that I had, O most Christian and very victorious King, since that my face, long obscured with cloud, presented itself before the deity of your measureless Majesty, since that in that I have been perpetually dazzled, never failing to honour and worthily revere that day, when first before it, as before a singularly humane majesty, I presented myself. I searched for some occasion by which to manifest good heart and frank courage, by the means of which I might grow into greater knowledge of your serene Majesty. I soon found in effect it was impossible for me to declare it, considering the contrast of the solitariness of my long obnubilation and obscurity, and my being suddenly thrust into brilliancy, and transported into the presence of the sovereign eye of the first monarch of the universe. Likewise I have long hung in doubt as to whom I ought to dedicate these three Centuries to, the remainder of my Prophecies amounting now to a thousand. I have long meditated on an act of such audacity. I have at last ventured to address your Majesty, and was not daunted from it as Plutarch, that grave author, relates in the life of Lycurgus, that, seeing the gifts and presents that were made in the way of sacrifice at the temples of the immortal gods in that age, many were staggered at the expense, and dared not approach the temple to present anything.

Notwithstanding this, I saw your royal splendour to be accompanied with an incomparable humanity, and paid my addresses to it, not as to those Kings of Persia whom it was not permissible to approach. But to a very prudent and very wise Prince I have dedicated my nocturnal and prophetic calculations, composed out of a natural instinct, and accompanied by a poetic fervour, rather than according to the strict rules of poetry. Most part, indeed, has been composed and adjusted by astronomical calculation corresponding to the years, months, and weeks, of the regions, countries, and for the most part towns and cities, throughout Europe, Africa, and a part of Asia, which nearest approach [or resemble] each other in all these climates, and this is composed in a natural manner. Possibly some may answer—who, if so, had better blow his nose [that he may see the clearer by it]—that the rhythm is as easy to be understood, as the sense is hard to get at. Therefore, O most gracious King, the bulk of the prophetic quatrains are so rude, that there is no making way through them, nor is there any interpreter of them. Nevertheless, being always anxious to set down the years, towns, and regions cited, where the events are to occur, even from the year 1585, and the year 1606, dating from the present time, which is the 14th of March, 1557.

Then passing far beyond to things which shall happen at the commencement of the seventh millenary, deeply calculated, so far as my astronomic calculus, and other knowledge, has been able to reach, to the time when the adversaries of Jesus Christ and of His Church shall begin to multiply in great force. The whole has been composed and calculated on days and hours of best election and disposition, and with all the accuracy I could attain to. At a moment [blessed] *"Minerva libera et non invita,"*[18] my calculations looking forward to events through a space of time to come that nearly equals that of the past even up to the present, and by this they will know in the lapse of time and in all regions what is to happen, all written down thus particularly, immingled with nothing superfluous.

Notwithstanding that some say, *"Quod de futuris non est determinata omnino veritas,"*[19] I will confess, Sire, that I believed myself capable of presage from the natural instinct I

18"When Minerva was free and favourable."
19"There can be no truth entirely determined for certain which concerns the future."

inherit of my ancestors, adjusted and regulated by elaborate calculation, and the endeavour to free the soul, mind, and heart from all care, solicitude, and anxiety, by resting and tranquilizing the spirit, which finally has all to be completed and perfected in one respect *tripode æneo* [by the brazen tripod]. With all this there will be many to attribute to me as mine, things no more mine than nothing. The Almighty alone, who strictly searches the human heart, pious, just, and pitiful, is the true Judge; to Him I pray to defend me from the calumny of wicked men. Such persons, with equal calumny, will bring into question how all your ancient progenitors the Kings of France have cured the evil; how those of other nations have cured the bite of serpents; others have had a certain instinct in the art of divination, and other faculties that would be too long to recount here. Notwithstanding such as cannot be restrained from the exercise of the malignancy of the evil spirit, [there is hope that] by the lapse of time, and after my extinction here on earth, my writings will be more valued than during my lifetime.

However, if I err in calculation of ages, or find myself unable to please all the world, may it please your Imperial Majesty to forgive me, for I protest before God and His saints, that I purpose to insert nothing whatever in writing this present Epistle that shall militate against the true Catholic Faith, whilst consulting the astronomical calculations to the very best of my knowledge. For the stretch of time of our forefathers [*i.e.* the age of the world] which has gone before is such, submitting myself to the direction of the soundest chronologists, that the first man, Adam, was about one thousand two hundred and forty years before Noah, not computing time by Gentile records, such as Varro has committed to writing, but taking simply the Sacred Scriptures for the guide in my astronomic reckonings, to the best of my feeble understanding.

After Noah, from him and the universal deluge, about one thousand and fourscore years, came Abraham, who was a sovereign astrologer according to some; he first invented the Chaldæan alphabet. Then came Moses, about five hundred and fifteen or sixteen years later. Between the time of David and Moses five hundred and seventy years elapsed. Then after the time of David and the time of our Saviour and Redeemer, Jesus Christ, born of a pure Virgin, there elapsed (according to some chronographers) one thousand three hundred and fifty years.

Some, indeed, may object to this supputation as not true, because it varies from that of Eusebius. Since the time of the human redemption to the hateful apostacy of the Saracens, there have been six hundred and twenty-one years, or thereabouts. Now, from this it is easy to gather what time has elapsed if my supputation be not good and available for all nations, for that all is calculated by the celestial courses, associated in my case with an emotion that steals over me at certain subsecival hours from an emotional tendency handed down to me from a line of ancestors. But the injuriousness of our time, O most serene Sovereign, requires that such secret events should not transpire, except in enigmatic sentences, having but one sense and one only meaning, and quite unmingled with calculation that is of ambiguity or amphibology. Say, rather, under a veiled obscurity from some natural emotional effusion, that resembles the sentential delivery of the thousand and two Prophets, that have been from the Creation of the world, according to the calculation and Punic Chronicle of Joel: *"Effundum spiritum meum super omnem carnem, et prophetabunt filii vestri, et filiæ vestræ."*[20] But this prophecy proceeded from the mouth of the Holy Spirit, which was the sovereign power eternal, in conjunction with the celestial

[20]See Joel ii. 28.

bodies, has caused some of the number to predict great and marvellous events.

As to myself in this place, I set up no claim to such a title —never, please God. I fully confess that all proceeds from God, and for that I return Him thanks, honour, and immortal praise, and have mingled nothing with it of the divination which proceeds *à fato,* but *à Deo, à naturâ,*[21] and for the most part accompanied with the movement of the celestial courses. Much as, if looking into a burning mirror [we see], as with darkened vision, the great events, sad or portentous, and calamitous occurrences that are about to fall upon the principal worshipers. First upon the temples of God, secondly upon such as have their support from the earth [*i.e.* by the kings], this decadence draweth nigh, with a thousand other calamitous incidents that in the course of time will be known to happen.

For God will take notice of the long barrenness of the great Dame, who afterwards will conceive two principal children. But, she being in great danger, the girl she will give birth to with risk at her age of death in the eighteenth year, and not possible to outlive the thirty-sixth, will leave three males and one female, and he will have two who never had any of the same father. The three brothers will be so different, though united and agreed, that the three and four parts of Europe will tremble. By the youngest in years will the Christian monarchy be sustained and augmented; heresies spring up and suddenly cast down, the Arabs driven back, kingdoms united, and new laws promulgated. Of the other children the first shall possess the furious crowned Lions, holding their paws upon the bold escutcheon. The second, accompanied by the Latins, shall penetrate so far that a second trembling and furious descent shall be made, descending Mons Jovis [at Barcelona] to

[21]Which proceeds from fate, but from God, and nature.

mount the Pyrenees, shall not be translated to the antique monarchy, and a third inundation of human blood shall arise, and March for a long while will not be found in Lent. The daughter shall be given for the preservation of the Christian Church, the dominator falling into the Pagan sect of new infidels, and she will have two children, the one fidelity, the other infidelity, by the confirmation of the Catholic Church. The other, who to his great confusion and tardy repentance wished to ruin her, will have three regions over a wide extent of leagues, that is to say, Roumania, Germany, and Spain, which will entail great intricacy of military handling, stretching from the 50th to the 52nd degree of latitude. And they will have to respect the more distant religions of Europe and the north above the 48th degree of latitude, which at first in a vain timidity will tremble, and then the more western, southern, and eastern will tremble. Their power will become such, that what is brought about by union and concord will prove insuperable by warlike conquest. By nature they will be equal, but exceedingly different in faith.

After this the sterile Dame, of greater power than the second, shall be received by two nations, by the first made obstinate by him who had power over all, by the second, and third, that shall extend his forces towards the circuit of the east of Europe; [arrived] there his standards will stop and succumb, but by sea he will run on to Trinacria and the Adriatic with his myrmidons. The Germans will succumb wholly and the Barbaric sect will be disquieted and driven back by the whole of the Latin race. Then shall begin the grand Empire of Antichrist in the Atila and Xerxes, [who is] to descend with innumerable multitudes, so that the coming of the Holy Spirit, issuing from the 48th degree, shall make a transmigration, chasing away the abomination of Antichrist, that made war upon the royal person of the great vicar of Jesus Christ, and against His Church, and reign *per tempus, et in occasione temporis* [for a time, and to the end of time]. This will be preceded by an eclipse of the sun, more obscure and tenebrose than has ever been since the creation of the world, up to the death and passion of Jesus Christ, and from thence till now. There will be in the month of October a grand revolution [translation] made, such that one would think that the librating body of the earth had lost its natural movement in the abyss of perpetual darkness. There will be seen precursive signs in the spring-time, and after extreme changes ensuing, reversal of kingdoms, and great earthquakes [*i.e.* wars]. All this accompanied with the procreations of the New Babylon [Paris], a miserable prostitute big with the abomination of the first holocaust [death of Louis XVI]. It will continue for only seventy-three years seven months.

Then there will issue from the stock so long time barren, proceeding from the 50th degree, [one] who will renovate the whole Christian Church. A great peace, union, and concord will then spring up between some of the children of races [long] opposed to each other and separated by diverse kingdoms. Such a peace shall be set up, that the instigator and promoter of military faction by means of the diversity of religions, shall dwell attached to the bottom of the abyss, and united to the kingdom of the furious, who shall counterfeit the wise. The countries, towns, cities, and provinces that had forsaken their old customs to free themselves, enthralling themselves more deeply, shall become secretly weary of their liberty, and, true religion lost, shall commence by striking off to the left, to return more than ever to the right.

Then replacing holiness, so long desecrated by their former writings [circulating slanders], afterwards the result will be that the great dog will issue as an irresistible mastiff [Napoleon?] who will destroy everything, even to all that may have been prepared in time past, till the churches will be restored as at first, and the clergy reinstated in their pristine condition; till it lapses again into whoredom and luxury, to commit and perpetrate a thousand crimes. And, drawing near to another desolation, then, when she shall be at her highest and sublimest point of dignity, the kings and generals [*mains militaires*] will come up [against her], and her two swords will be taken from her, and nothing will be left her but the semblance of them. [The following paragraphs I can make nothing of, so I give it in the words of Garencières and in inverted commas.] "From which by the means of the crookedness that draweth them, the people causing it to go straight, and not willing to submit unto them by the end opposite to the sharp hand that toucheth the ground they shall provoke." Until there shall be born unto the branch a long time sterile, one who shall deliver the French people from the benign slavery that they voluntarily submitted to, putting himself under the protection of Mars, and stripping Jupiter [Napoleon I.] of all his honours and dignities, for the city constituted free and seated in another narrow Mesopotamia. The chief and governor shall be cast from the midst, and set in a place of the air, ignorant of the conspiracy of the conspirators [Fouché, Duc d'Otranto, etc.] with the second Thrasibulus, who for a long time had prepared all this. Then shall the impurities and abominations be with great shame set forth and manifested to the darkness of the veiled light, shall cease towards the end of his reign, and the chiefs of the Church shall evince but little of the love of God, whilst many of them shall apostatize from the true faith.

Of the three sects [Lutheran, Catholic, and Mahometan], that which is in the middle, by the action of its own worshippers, will be thrown a little into decadence. The first totally throughout Europe, and the chief part of Africa exterminated by the third, by means of the poor in spirit, who by the madness engendered of libidinous luxury, will commit adultery [*i.e.* apostatize]. The people will pull down the pillar, and chase away the adherents of the legislators, and it shall seem, from the kingdoms weakened by the Orientals, that God the Creator has loosed Satan from the infernal prisons, to make room for the great Dog and Dohan [Gog and Magog], which will make so great and injurious a breach in the Churches, that neither the reds nor the whites, who are without eyes and without hands [meaning the latter Bourbons, "who learn nothing and forget nothing"], cannot judge of the situation, and their power will be taken from them. Then shall commence a persecution of the Church such as never was before. Whilst this is enacting, such a pestilence shall spring up that out of three parts of mankind two shall be removed. To such a length will this proceed that one will neither know nor recognize the fields or houses, and grass will grow in the streets of the cities as high as a man's knees. To the clergy there shall be a total desolation, and the martial men shall usurp what shall come back from the City of the Sun [Rome], and from Malta, and the Islands of Hières [off Marseilles], and the great chain of the port shall be opened that takes its name from the marine ox [Bosphorus].

A new incursion shall be made from the maritime shores, eager to give the leap of liberty since the first taking by the Mahometans. Their assaults shall not be at all in vain, and in the place where the habitation of Abraham was, it shall be assailed by those who hold the Jovialists [followers of Jupiter (Napoleon I. ?)] in reverence. The city of Achem [in the Island of Sumatra] shall be encompassed and assaulted on all sides by a great force of armed men. Their maritime forces shall be weakened by the Westerns. Upon this kingdom a great desolation shall come, and the great cities shall be depopulated, and such as enter in shall come under the vengeance of the wrath of God. The Holy Sepulchre, for so long a period an object of great veneration, shall remain exposed to the blighting dew of evening under the stars of heaven, and of the sun and moon. The holy place shall be converted into a stable for cattle small and large, and applied to other base purposes. Oh, what a calamitous time will that be for women with child! for then the Sultan of the East will be vanquished, driven for the most part by the Northern and Western men, who will kill him, overthrow him, and put the rest to flight, and his children, the offspring of many women, imprisoned. Then will come to its fulfilment the prophecy of the Royal Prophet, *"Ut audiret gemitus compeditorum, et solveret filios interemptorum."*[22]

What great oppression shall then fall upon the princes and rulers of kingdoms, even on those who are maritime and Oriental, their tongues intermingled from all nations of the earth! Tongues of the Latin nations, mingled with Arabic and North-African communication. All the Eastern kings will be driven away, overthrown, and exterminated, not at all by means of the kings of the North and the drawing near of our age, but by means of the three secretly united who seek out death and snares by ambush sprung upon one another. The renewal of this Triumvirate shall endure for seven years, while its renown shall spread all over the world, and the sacrifice of the holy and immaculate wafer shall be upheld. Then shall two lords of the North conquer the Orientals, and so great report and tumultuary warfare shall issue from these that all the East shall tremble at the noise of these two brothers of the North, who are yet not brothers. And because, Sire, by this discourse I almost introduce confusion into these predictions as to the time

---

[22]"Let the sighing of the prisoner come before thee, to release the children of death" (Ps. lxxviii. 11).

when the event of each shall fall out; for the detailed account of the time that follows is very little conformable, if at all, to what I gave above, that indeed could not err, being by astronomic rule and consonant with the Holy Scriptures themselves.

Had I wished to give to every quatrain its detailed date, it could easily have been done, but it would not have been agreeable to all, and still less to interpret them, Sire, until your Majesty should have fully sanctioned me to do this, in order not to furnish calumniators with an opportunity to injure me. Always reckoning the years since the creation of the world to the birth of Noah as being 1506 years, and from that to the completion of the building of the ark at the period of the universal deluge 600 years elapsed (let them be solar years, or lunar, or mixed), I hold that the Scripture takes them to be solar. At the conclusion of this 600 years, Noah entered the ark to escape the deluge. The deluge was universal over the earth, and lasted one year and two months. From the conclusion of the deluge to the birth of Abraham there elapsed 295 years, and 100 years from that to the birth of Isaac. From Isaac to Jacob 60 years. From the time he went into Egypt until his coming out of it was 130 years; and from the entry of Jacob into Egypt to his exit was 430 years; and from that to the building of the Temple by Solomon in the fortieth year of his reign, makes 480 years. From the building of the Temple to Jesus Christ, according to the supputation of the Hierographs, there passed 490 years. Thus by this calculation that I have made, collecting it out of the sacred writings, there are about 4173 years and eight months less or more. Now, from Jesus Christ, in that there is such a diversity of opinion, I pass it by, and having calculated the present prophecies in accordance with the order of the chain which contains the revolution, and the whole by astronomical rule, together with my own hereditary instinct. After some time, and including in it the period Saturn takes to turn between the 7th of April up to the 25th of August; Jupiter from the 14th of June to the 7th of October; Mars from the 17th of April to the 22nd of June; Venus from the 9th of April to the 22nd of May; Mercury from the 3rd of February to the 24th of the same; afterwards from the 1st of June to the 24th of the same; and from the 25th of September to the 16th of October, Saturn in Capricorn, Jupiter in Aquarius, Mars in Scorpio, Venus in Pisces, Mercury within a month in Capricorn, Aquarius, and Pisces; the moon in Aquarius, the Dragon's head in Libra, the tail in her sign opposite. Following the conjunction of Jupiter to Mercury, with a quadrin aspect of Mars to Mercury, and the head of the Dragon shall be with a conjunction of Sol with Jupiter, the year shall be peaceful without eclipse.

Then will be the commencement [of a period] that will comprehend in itself what will long endure [i.e. the vulgar advent of the French Revolution], and in its first year there shall be a great persecution of the Christian Church, fiercer than that in Africa [by the Vandals from 1439 to 1534], and this will burst out [durera] the year one thousand seven hundred and ninety-two; they will think it to be a renovation of time. After this the people of Rome will begin to reconstitute themselves [in 1804, when Napoleon is emperor], and to chase away the obscurity of darkness, recovering some share of their ancient brightness, but not without much division and continual changes. Venice after that, in great force and power, shall raise her wings very high, not much short of the force of ancient Rome. At that time great Byzantine sails, associated with the Piedmontese by the help and power of the North, will so restrain them that the two Cretans will not be able to maintain their faith. The arks built by the ancient warriors will accompany them to the waves of Neptune. In the Adriatic there will be such permutations, that what was united will be separated, and that will be reduced to a house which before was a great city, including the Pampotan and Mesopotamia of Europe, to 45, and others to 41, 42, and 47. And in that time and those countries the infernal power will set the power of the adversaries of its law against the Church of Jesus Christ. This will constitute the second Antichrist, which will persecute that Church and its true vicar, by means of the power of the temporal kings, who in their ignorance will be reduced by tongues that will cut more than any sword in the hands of a madman.

The said reign of Antichrist will last only to the death of him who was born near the [commencement] of the century, and of the other in the city of Plancus [Lyons], accompanied by him the elect of Modena, Fulcy by Ferara, upheld by the Adriatic Piedmontese, and the proximity of the great Trinacria [Sicily]. Afterwards the Gallic Ogmion shall pass the Mount Jovis [Barcelona], accompanied by so great a number that from afar the Empire shall be presented with its grand law, and then and for some time after shall be profusely shed the blood of the innocent by the guilty recently elevated to power. Then by great deluges the memory of things contained in such instruments shall suffer incalculable loss, even to the Alphabet itself. This will happen among the Northerns. By the Divine Will once again Satan will be bound, and universal peace established amongst mankind, and the Church of Jesus Christ delivered from all tribulation, although the Azostains [debauched voluptuaries] would desire to mix with the honey the gall of their pestilent seduction. This will be near the seventh millenary, when the sanctuary of Jesus Christ will no longer be trodden down by the infidels who come from the North; the world [will be then] approaching its great conflagration, although by my supputation in my prophecies, the course of time runs much farther on.

In the epistle that some years since I dedicated to my son Cæsar Nostradamus, I have openly enough declared some points without presage. But here, Sire, are comprised many great and marvellous events to come, which those who follow after us shall see. And during the said astrological supputation, harmonized with the sacred Scriptures, the persecution of the Ecclesiastics shall take its rise in the power of the kings of the North, united with the Easterns. And this persecution shall last eleven years, or somewhat less, by which time the chief Northern king shall pass away, which years being run, a united Southern king shall succeed, which shall still more fiercely persecute the clergy of the Church for the space of three years by the Apostolical seduction of one who will take away all the absolute power from the Church Militant, and holy people of God who observe its ritual, and the whole order of religion shall be greatly persecuted and so afflicted that the blood of true ecclesiastics shall float everywhere. To one of those horrible temporal kings such praise shall be given by his adherents that he will have shed more human blood of innocent ecclesiastics, than any could do of wine. This king will commit crimes against the Church that are incredible. Human blood will flow in the public streets and churches, like water after impetuous rain, and will crimson with blood the neighbouring rivers, and by another naval war redden the sea to such a degree that one king shall say to another, *"Bellis rubuit navalibus æquor."*[23] Then in the same year and those following there will ensue the most horrible pestilence and the most astonishing on account of the famine that will precede, and such tribulation that nothing approaching it ever happened since the

[23]"The sea blushed red with the blood of naval fights."

first foundation of the Christian Church; this also throughout all the Latin regions, leaving traces in all the countries under the rule of Spain.

Then the third King of the North [Russia?], hearing the complaint of the people from [whom he derives] his principal title, will raise up a mighty army, and pass through the limits [*destroits*] of his last progenitors and great-grandfathers, to him who will [*qui* for *lui qui*] replace almost everything in its old condition. The great Vicar of the Cope shall be put back to his pristine state; but, desolated and abandoned by all, will return to the sanctuary [that was] destroyed by Paganism, when the Old and New Testament will be thrust out and burnt. After that Antichrist will be the infernal prince. Then at this last epoch, all the kingdoms of Christianity, as well as of the infidel world, will be shaken during the space of twenty-five years, and the wars and battles will be more grievous, and the towns, cities, castles, and all other edifices will be burnt, desolated, and destroyed with much effusion of vestal blood, married women and widows violated, sucking children dashed and broken against the walls of towns; and so many evils will be committed by means of Satan, the prince infernal, that nearly all the world will become undone and desolated. Before the events occur certain strange birds [imperial eagles] will cry in the air, *"To-day! to-day!"* and after a given time will disappear [June, 1815]. After this has endured for a certain length of time [twenty-five years he has said before, 1790 to 1815], there will be almost renewed another reign of Saturn, the age of gold [this might be the discovery of California, but for what follows]. God the Creator shall say, hearing the affliction of His people, Satan shall be precipitated and bound in the bottomless abyss, and then shall commence between God and men a universal peace. There he shall abide for the space of a thousand years, and shall turn his greatest force against the power of the Church, and shall then be bound again.

How justly are all these figures adapted by the divine letters to visible celestial things, that is to say, by Saturn, Jupiter, and Mars, and others in conjunction with them, as may be seen more at large by some of the quatrains! I would have calculated it more deeply, and adapted the one to the other; but, seeing, O most serene King, that some who are given to censure will raise a difficulty, I shall take the opportunity to retire my pen and seek my nocturnal repose. *"Multa etiam, O Rex potentissime præclara, et sane in brevi ventura, sed omnia in hâc tuâ Epistola, innectere non possumus, nec volumus, sed ad intellegenda quædam facta, horrida fata pauca libanda sunt, quamvis tanta sit in omnes tua amplitudo et humanitas homines, deosque pietas, ut solos amplissimo et Christianissimo Regis nomine, et ad quem summa totius religionis auctoritas deferatur dignus esse videare."*[24] But I shall only beseech you, O most clement King, by this your singular and most prudent goodness, to understand rather the desire of my heart, and the sovereign wish I have to obey your most excellent Majesty, ever since my eyes approached so nearly to your solar splendour, than the grandeur of my work can attain to or acquire.

> *Faciebat* MICHAEL NOSTRADAMUS.
> *Solonæ Petræ Provinciæ.*

From Salon this 27th June, 1558.

[24]"Many things, O most potent king of all, of the most remarkable kind are shortly to happen, that I neither could nor would interweave them all into this epistle; but in order to comprehend certain facts, a few horrible destinies must be set down in extract, although your amplitude and humanity towards all men is so great, and your piety to the gods, that you alone seel. worthy of the grand title of the most Christian King, and to whom the highest authority in all religion should be deferred."

ABOUT THIS TRANSLATION

This collection of quatrains from the *Centuries* has benefitted from research involving many translations, including the first English edition of Garencieres in 1672. Due to the enigmatic style and content, and the effort by translators to adjust predictions to events within their own time, translations vary considerably. This edition includes a brief italicized statement, often giving the opinions of noted Nostradamus interpreters, to assist the reader in understanding the import of each quatrain.

Most of the thousand quatrains deal with events in France, the author's native land, or historical events which have occurred during the four hundred years since his death. While many of them are significant from the standpoint of his accuracy, only those which deal with the future or which seem as yet unfulfilled are included here.

Proper names have not been changed, remaining in the disguised anagram form of the original. The lines have been rephrased into modern English for better understanding, but with great care not to change meaning or emphasis. If they seem vague and unintelligible, that is how Nostradamus wrote them and how he intended them to be. Readers who would like to see all thousand quatrains can find complete editions in larger public libraries. It is recommended that at least two different versions be consulted.

Nostradamus

I. 16

When Saturn is in Aquarius,
And Sagittarius is ascendant
Disease, famine, and death by war
As the century approaches renewal

[*Wollner sees 1699 AD, Roberts sees
1999 AD*]

I. 24

Condemnation considered in the new city
The bird of prey submits itself to judgment
Prisoners are pardoned after victory
Cremona and Mantua have suffered greatly

[*Nuremberg war trials?*]

I. 29

When the fish which is of land and sea
Is beached in a strong sea
With strange and powerful form
The enemy will be at the walls by the sea

[*D-Day, World War II?*]

I. 31

The war in France will last many years
Beyond the influence of the Spanish King
Uncertain victory crowns three great ones
The Eagle, Cock, Moon, Lion, in the Sun

[*U. S., France, China, England after
World War II?*]

I. 38

The Sun and Eagle will both be victorious
By vain reply the vanquished are assured
But armaments will continue
Revenge and war deaths will bring peace

[*Religion and the state join to stop wars?*]

I. 48

When twenty years of the moon's reign pass
Seven thousand years, another will hold
  dominion
When the sun resumes its waning days
My prophecy will be fulfilled and finished

[*Some see the end of the world here*]

I. 50

From the aquatic triplicity will be born
One who makes Thursday his holiday
Its fame, praise, rule, and power will grow
By land and sea to become a force to the East

[*Emergence of the U. S. as a world power?*]

I. 51

Jupiter and Saturn join in the head of Aries
Eternal God, what changes!
After awhile evil times return
Gaul and Italy, what unrest!

[*Wollner sees Sept. 2, 1995; Norab sees
  Sept. 12, 1994*]

I. 63

The scourge passes, the world shrinks,
There is lasting peace, population increases,
One will travel by air, land, and sea
And wars will begin again and again

[*Most interpret the 20th century*]

I. 64

They will think they see the sun at night
As the pig-half man is seen
Noise, song, combat, battles in the sky,
And brutish beasts heard talking

[*Modern warfare or riots in the streets?*]

I. 68

What horrible and sad torment
Three innocent ones seeking deliverance
Poison suspected, guards will betray them
Horror comes to them by drunk executioners

[*Death of the Romanovs July 16, 1918?*]

III. 31

I. 76

He will be called by a wild name
So that the three sisters will have destiny's
　　name
He will lead a great people by word and deed
He will have fame and renown above all
　　others

[*No clear consensus*]

I. 81

Nine are set aside from the human flock
Divided in their judgment and counsel
Their destiny is to be divided
Kappa, Theta, Lambda dead, banished, lost

[*Supreme Court? What does the last line
mean?*]

I. 84

The moon will be obscured by darkness
Her brother passes in rust color
The great one hidden long in the shadows
Will cool his sword in blood

[*Moon eclipsed, sun red, a great one comes*]

I. 87

Neptune shakes fire from the earth's center
Causing a great earthquake in the new city
Two great rocks make war a long time
Then Arethusa makes a new river red

[*Boswell interprets New York destroyed*]

I. 100

For a long time a gray bird is seen in the sky
Near Dole and the Tuscan land
In its beak a green twig
Soon a great one will die and the war will end

[*The death of Franklin Roosevelt?*]

II. 9

For nine years the vegetarian keeps the peace
Then he falls into such bloody thirst
The great people die without faith or law
He will be killed by one more debonair

[*Some see Louis XVI, others the future*]

II. 28

The greatest of the Prophet's surname
Will take Monday for his sabbath
He will wander far due to a troubled mind
Delivering a great people from oppression

[*No clear consensus*]

II. 41

The great star will burn seven days
A cloud makes two suns appear
The big mastiff howls all night
A great pope will change his country

[*Roberts sees Pius XII; Leoni feels suns may
be nuclear explosions*]

II. 43

During the time of the bearded star
Three great princes will become enemies
Struck from the sky, the earth trembles
Po, Tiber overflow, snakes are cast ashore

[*Roberts sees Halley's comet 1985; Leoni
sees the 16th century*]

II. 48

The great force will pass over mountains
Saturn in Sagittarius; Mars to Pisces
Poison hidden in the heads of salmon
The warrior chief hanged with cord

[*Leoni predicts July 13, 2193*]

II. 70

The dart from heaven ends its circuit
Some die in mid-speech, a great killing
Stone in the tree, a proud nation humbled
Noise, a human monster, purged by expiation

[*Roberts sees World War II rockets*]

II. 71

The exiles come to Sicily
Deliverance from hunger and foreign
    control
In the dawn the Celts fail them
Life preserved by reason, the king enjoins

[*The Jews founding Israel despite British
    indifference?*]

II. 75

The sound of a rare bird will be heard
On the pipe of the highest story
The bushel of wheat will rise so high
That man will eat his fellow man

[*Supersonic aircraft and overproduction?*]

II. 89

One day, two great masters will be friends
Their great power will increase
The new land will reach its peak
Their powers told to the bloody one

[*Churchill and Roosevelt? U.S. and
    Europe?*]

II. 90

Life and death change the realm of Hungary
The law more severe than service
Wailing and weeping in their great city
Castor and Pollux enemies in the arena

[*Hungarian revolt of 1956?*]

II. 91

A great fire will be seen as the sun rises
Noise and light extending far northward
Death and cries are heard within the circle
Death by iron, fire, famine awaiting them

[*Leoni sees World War III*]

II. 97

Roman Pontiff, beware of coming
To the city where two rivers flow
Your blood will spurt near there
You and yours when the rose blooms

[*A pope killed in a city of two rivers?*]

II. 100

There will be horrible tumult within the isles
Only the sounds of war will be heard
The assault of the plunderers so great
That they join together into a great legion

[*Battle of Britain, World War II?*]

III. 2

The divine word will give to the substance
Heaven and earth, gold hid in mystic deed
Body, soul, spirit, having all power
As much underfoot as is heavenly seen

[*Spiritual awareness yet to come?*]

III. 13

Gold and silver melted by lightning in the ark
Of two captives, one will eat the other
The greatest one of the city hanged
When the once submerged fleet swims

[*Submarines in line 4 but what of the rest?*]

III. 16

An English prince, Mars in heavenly heart
Will want to follow his prosperous future
Of two duels, one will pierce his gall
Resented by him, loved by his mother

[*Duke of Windsor, formerly Edward
    VIII?*]

IV. 15

III. 31

On the fields of Media, Arabia, Armenia
Two great armies meet three times
The host near the shore of Araxes
Will fall in the land of Solomon

[*Roberts sees battle in the Near East with
    Jews suffering*]

III. 34

When there is an eclipse of the Sun
The monster will be seen at noon
It will be interpreted otherwise
Unfortunate, for none will foresee it

[*Rise of communism?*]

III. 36

Buried, apoplectic, but not dead
He will be found with hands consumed
When the city condemns the heretic
Who they believed changed their laws

[*Roberts sees Hitler escaping Berlin!*]

III. 63

The Roman power will be forcibly defeated
His great neighbor will follow in his
 footsteps
Secret and civil hate and conflicts
Will stop the buffoon's follies

[*Many see Mussolini and Hitler*]

III. 77

The third climate completed under Aries
The year 2025 (1727?), in October (27th?)
The King of Persia captured by those of
 Egypt
Conflict, death, loss, the cross shamed

[*Roberts sees October 27, 2025*]

III. 78

A Scottish chief with six of Germany
Will be captured by Eastern sailors
They will pass through Gibraltar and Spain
And present him to the feared new King in
 Persia

[*Continuation of III. 77*]

III. 86

An Italian chief will sail to Spain
He will stop at Marseilles
He lingers a long time before he dies
After his death, a great wonder is seen

[*Most agree this still lies in the future*]

III. 92

The world near its last period
Saturn again late, will come back
Dominion changed to the black nations
The age plucked by the hawk at Narbonne

[*Black nations to dominate the world?*]

III. 95

The law of Moor (More?) will decline
Followed by another more seductive
The Dnieper will give way first
The other succeeds by pardon and voice

[*Decline of communism starting in
Ukraine?*]

III. 96

The chief of Fossan will have his throat cut
By the leader of bloodhound and greyhound
The deed is by those of the Tarpeian Rock
Saturn in Leo, February 13th

[*Wollner sees 1977, 2007, 2036, 2066, 2095,
    2124, or 2154 A.D.*]

III. 97

New law will prevail in the new land
Towards Syria, Judea, and Palestine
The great barbarian empire declines
Before the moon completes its cycle

[*Wollner sees 2080, 2332 A.D.; Leoni sees
    1917-20; Roberts sees fall of the Arab Con-
    federacy*]

IV. 5

The cross and peace under the divine word
Spain and France will unite together
Bitter conflict and a near disaster
No heart so strong as not to tremble

[*Leoni sees the Antichrist*]

IV. 11

He who governs by the great cloak
Will be induced to perform acts
Twelve red ones will stain the cloth
Murder will be perpetrated

[*Cardinals betray a pope, a popular Nostradamus theme*]

IV. 15

Where they sought to make famine come
From there will come plenty
The eye of the sea through animal greed
One for the other gives oil and wheat

[*England, U-boats, U. S. aid in World War
II?*]

IV. 18

Some of the most learned in celestial science
Will be condemned by ignorant leaders
Punished by edict, hunted as criminals
Put to death wherever they are found

[*Leoni sees a persecution of astrologers*]

IV. 23

The legion in the marine fleet
Will burn lime, oxides, sulfur, pitch
A long pause in the secure place
Port Selin and Monaco consumed by fire

[*Roberts sees chemical warfare*]

IV. 25

An infinity of celestial bodies visible to the
    eye
For this reason will be clouded, obscured
Body and brain, sense and head invisible
Diminishing the sacred prayers

[*Pelletier sees science weakening religion*]

IV. 28

When Venus is covered by the Sun
A hidden form will be under the splendor
Mercury will expose them to the fire
By warlike noise it will be provoked

[*Garencieres sees the "philosopher's stone"*]

IV. 29

The Sun will be eclipsed by Mercury
It will be second in the sky
By Vulcan, Hermes will become food
The Sun pure, radiant red and gold

[*Most agree this contines IV. 28*]

IV. 32

In places and times, flesh will give way to fish
Communal law will oppose this
The old support it, then removed from the
   milieu
Love of everything in common is set aside

[*Larmor sees the decline of communism*]

IV. 50

Libra will see the West dominate
Holding dominion over heaven and earth
No one will see the Asian forces perish
Only seven hold the hierarchy in order

[*Leoni sees Spanish or U. S. popes or
   H-bombs!*]

V. 18

IV. 85

The white coal will be chased by the black
one
Made prisoner and carried away in a dung
cart
Black camel on twisted feet
The youngest will blind the pet falcon

[*Roberts sees white leader killed by black
leader*]

IV. 96

The oldest sister of the British isle
Will be born 15 years after her brother
By her promise and her truth
She succeeds to kingdom of the balance

[*Roberts sees the U. S. as brother (1776) and
France as sister (1791)*]

V. 8

Unending fire will bring hidden death
Horrible and fearful within the globes
The fleet will destroy the city at night
The city will burn, the enemy pleased

[*A horrible new weapon?*]

V. 18

The unhappy abandoned one dies of grief
Beaten by a woman who celebrates the
    hecatomb
Pristine law and free edicts drawn up
The law and the Prince fall the 7th day

[*Apparently a woman leader yet to come*]

V. 26

The Slavic People by luck in war
Are elevated to a very high level
They change their ruler, one born provincial,
An army raised in mountains to cross the sea

[*Rise of communism and the Soviet
    Union?*]

V. 32

Where all is well the Sun is good
The Moon is full, but ruin is near
From the sky your fortune changes
In the same state as the seventh rock

[*War between Catholics and Protestants —
    Ireland?*]

V. 36

The sister's brother, by quarrel and deceit
Will mix dew in the mineral
On a cake given to a slow old woman
She dies tasting it, simple, crude

[*A woman leader poisoned?*]

V. 46

Quarrels and new schisms by the red hats
When the Sabine is elected
They will produce great sophisms against
   him
Rome will be injured by the Albanois

[*Most see a pope elected amid disunity*]

V. 49

Not from Spain but from France
One will be elected for St. Peter's Bark
A promise made to an enemy
Will cause cruel plague in his realm

[*A French Pope?*]

V. 56

By the death of the very old Pontiff
A Roman of good age is elected
It will be said he weakens the see
But he lives long and acts courageously

[*Old pope succeeded by an active younger
one?*]

V. 62

It will rain blood on the rocks
Sun in the East, Saturn in the West
War near Orgon, great evil at Rome
Ships sunk, ruler of the seas taken

[*Leoni sees Christianity as Sun, Antichrist as
Saturn; Roberts sees war between Orient
and Occident*]

V. 75

He will rise high, more to the right
He will remain seated on the square stone
Towards the South, facing to the left
The crooked staff in hand, his mouth shut

[*One of the most enigmatic of all quatrains!*]

V. 83

Those who have planned subversion
On the great, invincible, unequalled
     kingdom
Will act by deceit, with three nights' warning
While the great one reads a Bible at the table

[*Communist conspiracy?*]

V. 92

After the seat is held seventeen years
Five will change within the same time
Then one is elected at the same time
He will not be acceptable to the Romans

[*Succession of many popes after one serves
17 years, then an unpopular one?*]

V. 95

The nautical oar will invite shadows
Then it will stir up the great empire
Wooden obstacles in the Aegean Sea
Obstructing the flow of the Tyrrhenian Sea

[*Some future feat of engineering?*]

V. 98

At the 48th climacteric degree
At the end of Cancer, a great drought
Fish boiled hectic in sea, river, and lake
Bearn and Bigorre distressed by heavenly fire

[*A great heat spell and drought?*]

VI. 2

In the year 580, more or less
There will be a strange era
In the year 703 the heavens will witness
Several kingdoms, one to five, changed

[*Roberts sees 2028 A.D.*]

VI. 6

Towards the North there will appear
A comet, not far from Cancer
Susa, Siena, Boetia, Eretria
The great one of Rome dies, overnight

[*No clear consensus*]

VI. 8

Those recognized for their learning
Become poor at the change of a King
Some exiled, without help, without gold
The lettered and letters of little value

[*Persecution of scholars or high professional
unemployment at change of govern-
ment?*]

VI. 10

In a little while temples of colors
Of white and black intermixed
Red and yellow withdraw from them
Blood, land, plague, famine, fire, destroy
them

[*Leoni sees monastic orders; Roberts sees
interracial strife*]

VI. 17

After the books are burned
The asses change their clothes
The Saturnines burned by the millers
Except the greater part will be bared

[*Intellectuals attacked by the masses?*]

VI. 10

VI. 19

The true flame will consume the lady
Who will want to burn the Innocents
Before the attack the army is encouraged
A beefy monster is seen at Seville

[*Leoni sees bullfight omen; Roberts sees a
    real monster*]

VI. 21

When those of the Arctic Pole are united
Great fear and terror in the East
The newly elected calms the unrest
Rhodes, Byzantium, stained by Barbarian
    blood

[*No clear consensus*]

VI. 22

Within the land of the heavenly temple
During a feigned peace a nephew is murdered
The bark will become schismatic
False liberty proclaimed everywhere

[*Intrigue, murder, civil-religious unrest?*]

VI. 24

Mars and the Sceptre in conjunction
Under Cancer, there will be a chaotic war
Soon after, a new king anointed
One who brings peace for a long time

[*Wollner sees June 21, 2002*]

VI. 34

The invention of aimed flying fire
Will greatly trouble the besieged chief
There will be much sedition within
The abandoned will despair

[*A modern theme of guided missiles and
subversion*]

VI. 35

Near the Bears, towards the white wool,
Aries, Taurus, Cancer, Leo, Virgo
Mars, Jupiter, The Sun burns a great plain
Woods and cities, letters hidden in the candle

[*Leoni sees a great drought; Roberts sees a
worldwide raging fire*]

VI. 50

Within the pit, bones will be found
The stepmother will commit incest
The state changed, they demand fame and
    praise
And Mars will be the attending star

[*No clear consensus*]

VI. 66

At the forming of a new sect
The bones of a great Roman are found
The sepulchre covered by marble appears
Not well buried, an earthquake in April

[*No clear consensus; seems yet to come*]

VI. 97

At 450 the heavens will burn
The fire nears the great new city
In an instant a great flame leaps upward
When one demands proof of the Normans

[*Boswell sees Halifax October 6, 1917;
    Roberts sees major city burned in the
    future*]

VI. 98

Ruin for the Volcae will be very frightful
Their great city tainted, pestilential fate
Plunder of gold and silver, temples violated
And two rivers red with flowing blood

[*Roberts sees Hiroshima*]

VI. 99

The learned enemy will be confused
Disease in his camp, defeated by ambush
The Pyrenees and Pennine Alps denied him
Discovery of ancient urns near the river

[*No clear consensus*]

VII. 2

By Mars, Aries will not give battle
The soldiers are surprised at night
On land, Black and White hiding indigo
Traitors seen under feigned shadow

[*No clear consensus*]

VII. 5

Some of the wine on the table will spill
The third one will not have what he claimed
The black one of Parma twice descended
Will do to Perugia and Pisa what he believed

[*No clear consensus*]

VII. 14

They will expose false topography
The tomb urns will be opened
Sects and holy philosophy multiply
Black for white, new for old

[*Pelletier sees 16th century France, Roberts
sees corruption in future*]

VII. 18

The besieged will color their agreements
Seven days after a crucial issue
Repulsed, fire, blood, seven axed
Captive, a lady who tried to make peace

[*A turning point in a war, but past or
future?*]

VII. 28

The captain will lead a great troop
Near the enemy on the mountain
Surrounded by fire he finds his path
All escape except 30 put on the spit

[*No clear consensus*]

VII. 31

More than 10,000 from Languedoc and
    Guienne
Will again want to pass over the Alps
The Great Saroyans march against Brundis
Aquin and Bresse will drive them back

[*No clear consensus*]

VII. 32

From a Montreal cottage will be born
One very clever who will tyrannize
He will organize forces in Milan
To drain Fauene and Florence of gold and
    men

[*Roberts sees a humbly born Canadian
    leader*]

VII. 36

God, Heaven, all divine words in waters
Carried by seven red shaved heads to
    Byzantium
Against the anointed 300 from Trebizond
Will establish two laws, horror, then belief

[*Seven cardinals or priests against 300 non-
    believers from Constantinople?*]

VII. 37

Ten will be sent to execute the ship's captain
Warned by one, the fleet in open warfare
Confusion as the chiefs prick and bite
The Rhine, Hyeres, within the north cape

[*Leoni sees an admiral assassinated, Roberts
    sees a mutiny in the German navy*]

VII. 39

The leader of the French army
Thinking to rout the principal phalanx
On the pavement of oats and slate
Foreigners subverting Genoa

[*No clear consensus*]

VII. 41

VII. 40

In empty drums smeared with oil and grease
Twenty-one shut up, before the port
At second watch facing death they do their
    deed
To win the gates and die by the watch

[*21 men in a sneak attack, but past or
    future?*]

VII. 41

The bones of feet and hands shackled
Noise causes the house to be uninhabited a
    long time
Dreams cause them to be dug up
The house again healthy, inhabited, without
    noise

[*Garencieres sees Lapacodier in 1624,
    Roberts sees a haunted house*]

VII. 73

Sieges worsened by plunder and corruption
The holy one charged, passing over the
    sermon
Imprisoned, captives held in triple fields
One from the deepest depths raised to the
    throne

[*No clear consensus*]

VII. 80

The West will be free of the British
The recognized one passes low then high
The discontented Scottish rebel
Rebels more in the warm nights

[*Many see John Paul Jones, 1778*]

VIII. 5

A brightly adorned temple will appear
The lamp and candle at Borne and Breteuil
The Canton of Lucerne is turned away
When the great Cock is seen in his tomb

[*Leoni sees discovery of ancient temple*]

VIII. 10

A great stench issues from Lausanne
Such that no one knows its source
They will exile all foreigners
Fire in the heavens, strangers defeated

[*Leoni sees Calvinists or Communists,
    Roberts sees a peace treaty that fails*]

VIII. 14

Great credit and abundant gold and silver
Honor will be blinded by lust
The offense of the adulterer will be known
It will bring great dishonor

[*Leoni sees 16th century, Roberts sees future
   inflation and loose morals*]

VIII. 16

Where Jason had his ship built
Will be a great and sudden flood
So one has no place or land to go to
The waves climb Olympian Fesulan

[*A flood, but past or future?*]

VIII. 17

The affluent will suddenly be put down
Three brothers plunge the world into
   trouble
Enemies will seize the maritime city
Famine, fire, flood, plague, all evils doubled

[*Pelletier sees the French Revolution,
   Roberts sees a future world revolution*]

VIII. 19

To maintain the great troubled cloak
The reds will march to clear it
A family almost ruined by death
The red reds strike down the red one

[*Conspiracy of cardinals again or Kennedy
family and USSR-China split?*]

VIII. 20

False message about a fraudulent election
Is stopped from circulating through the city
Voices bought, chapel tainted with blood
The empire goes to another

[*Leoni sees civil war, Roberts sees a crisis in
the church*]

VIII. 41

A fox will be elected saying nothing
Playing saint publicly, feathering his nest
   privately
Afterwards he will suddenly tyrannize
His foot will be on the throats of the greatest

[*A common phenomenon of political
ambition and intrigue*]

VIII. 55

He finds himself trapped between two rivers
Barrels and casks joined together to pass over
Eight bridges down, the chief imprisoned
Perfect children will have their throats cut

[*No clear consensus*]

VIII. 63

The adulterer will be wounded without a
    blow
He murders his wife and son for spite
Wife knocked down, the child strangled
Eight captives taken, choked without respite

[*No clear consensus*]

VIII. 71

The number of astronomers will be so great
Driven out, banished, their books burned
In 1607 by a consecrated assemblage
So none will be safe from the Holy ones

[*Inquisition persecutes astrologers?*]

VIII. 79

He born of a nunnery, father killed by iron
Will conceive anew in Gorgon's blood
Will in foreign land do all to keep silent
He will burn himself and child

[*No clear consensus*]

VIII. 90

When one of the crusaders, of troubled mind
Will see a horned ox in a holy place
Will his place be filled by a virgin pig
Order no longer sustained by the king

[*No clear consensus*]

VIII. 93

Seven months and he is no longer Prelate
By his death a great schism arises
Seven months another is governor
Peace near Venice, unity comes again

[*A Pope, then a leader dies, disunity, then
unity once again?*]

VIII. 96

The Synagogues sterile, without fruit,
Will be received by the infidels
The daughter of the persecuted Babylonians
Will have her wings clipped, sadness, misery

*[Boswell sees Jewish conversion of Islam,
others see decline or persecution of Jews]*

VIII. 98

The blood of religions will flow freely
In great abundance, like water
It will not cease for a long time
Woe, ruin and hardship to the clergy

[Decline of religion, but past or future?]

IX. 7

He who will open the discovered tomb
Will not close it again promptly
Evil comes to him, no one can disprove
Whether it is better to be British or Norman
  King

*[Opening of King Tut's tomb, or a future
  discovery?]*

VIII. 14

IX. 10

The child of a monk and nun exposed, dead
Killed by a bear, carried off by a boar
The army camped at Foix and Pamiers
Carcassone organizes against Toulouse

[*Decline of religion?*]

IX. 11

The just will be executed
Publicly and in secret
Great pestilence comes to the place
So that the judges have to flee

[*Continuation of IX. 10?*]

IX. 16

From Castelfranco the assembly comes
The displeased ambassador creates schism
Those of the Riviera argue
And deny entry into the great gulf

[*Leoni sees Castelfranco as a place, Roberts
sees Franco, the man*]

IX. 31

An earthquake will strike Mortara
The islands of St. George half sunk
War awakens the sleepy peace
Abysses ripped open in the temple at Easter

[*Leoni sees a statue toppled or all of Britain
    sinking*]

IX. 34

The receptive, docile one will be mitred
Returns conflict, passing over the tiles
One traitor betrays 500 and is titled
Narbonne and Saulce oil their knives

[*A famous quatrain. Louis XVI wore a red
    mitre and was betrayed by Narbonne, his
    minister of war, and Saulce, mayor of Va-
    rennes*]

IX. 44

Leave, leave Geneva, all of you!
Saturn will change gold into iron
Raypoz will kill all who oppose
The heavens show signs beforehand

[*Pelletier sees Paris, Leoni sees Calvinist
    Geneva, Roberts sees atomic power!*]

IX. 48

The great maritime city of the Ocean
Environment of marshes and crystal
In winter solstice and in spring
Will be tried by a fearful wind

[*Hurricane? Allen sees Central Park, Boswell sees Tokyo, Roberts sees London*]

IX. 53

The young Nero in three chimneys
Will cause pages to be burnt alive
Happy are those far from such deeds
Three of his blood will have him killed

[*No clear consensus*]

IX. 55

A horrible war prepared in the West
A year later pestilence comes
So horrible that young, old, nor beast escape
Blood, fire Mercury, Mars, Jupiter, in France

[*Jaubert sees 16th century, Leoni sees 20th century*]

IX. 48

IX. 66

There will be peace, unity, and change
For estates, offices, the lowly and the high
To prepare a journey torment is the first fruit
Wars will cease by legal process and debates

[*Post-war period, but which war?*]

IX. 70

Sharp weapons will be hid in flaming torches
In Lyons, the day of the Sacrament
The Viennese, every one, cut to pieces
By the Latin cantons, as Mascon truly said

[*A local event or modern global warfare?*]

IX. 72

The holy temples will be polluted once again
Plundered by the Toulouse Senate
Saturn two three cycle revolutions
In April, May, people of new leaven

[*Leoni sees Calvinist-Catholic strife, Roberts
    sees religious revolution in 2150 A.D.*]

IX. 76

With the bloody and rapacious black one
Descended from the lust bed of inhuman
  Nero
Between two rivers, by the military left hand
Murdered by a bald youth

[*All ponder the "new" Nero and the exact
  city*]

IX. 83

The earth trembles terribly Sun 20th of
  Taurus
The great theatre, crowded, will be ruined
The air, sky, earth, obscured and troubled
Then the infidel calls on God and the saints

[*A great catastrophe April 20th or May
  10th*]

IX. 99

The Aquilon Wind will cause the siege to be
  lifted
Ashes, lime, and dust thrown over walls
Rain later does them much worse
The last hope against the frontier

[*Aquilon is Latin for North or North Wind;
  could it mean the U.S.S.R.?*]

IX. 100

Night is overcome in a great sea battle
Fire in the Western ships, then ruin
A new tactic, the great ship colored
Anger to the vanquished, victory in mist

[*Camouflage and modern naval warfare?*]

X. 9

On a misty day in the Figueres Castle
A sovereign prince is born to an infamous
    woman
Born after his father's death, surname of
    breeches
Never was a king so bad in his province

[*Leoni sees Antichrist, Roberts sees a tyrant*]

X. 10

Stained by murder and many adulteries
A great enemy of the whole human race
Worse than his grandfather, uncles, their
    fathers
In iron, fire, water, bloody and inhuman

[*Continuation of X. 9?*]

X. 11

At the dangerous passage below Ionchere
Posthumously his band passes
Over the Pyrenees with his belongings
The duke rushes from Parpignan to Tende

[*Continuation of X. 10?*]

X. 15

Aged father duke will be very thirsty
When his son denies him in his extremity
Into the well alive but coming up dead
The fatherly Senate has the son executed

[*No clear consensus*]

X. 42

Humane realm and angelic offspring
Causes lasting peace and unity
War subdues under its control
Peace is maintained for a long time

[*Pax Britannica, U.S., or future?*]

X. 49

Garden of the World near the new city
In the path of hollow mountains
Seized and plunged into the vat
Forced to drink water poisoned by sulfur

[*Leoni sees Vesuvius, Boswell Palisades in
New Jersey and "hollow mountain" sky-
scrapers; natural disaster or pollution?*]

X. 67

An earthquake in the month of May
Saturn in Capricorn; Jupiter, Mercury in
   Taurus
Venus in Cancer; Mars in Virgo
Hail falls larger than an egg

[*Wollner sees May 3755, others see May
10th in an unknown year*]

X. 72

In the seventh month of 1999
A great king of Terror comes from the sky
To receive the king of Angolmois
Before and after, Mars reigns by good
   fortune

[*Angolmois could be Mongols or the spirit
of Genghis Khan*]

X. 42

X. 73

The present together with the past
Judges by the great Jovialist
The world tires of him at last
Judged disloyal by the Clergy

[*Continuation of X. 72? Roberts sees
Rabelais*]

X. 74

The year of the great seventh number passed
An apparition at time of ritual sacrifice
Not far from the age of the millennium
When the buried go out from their tombs

[*No clear consensus*]

X. 75

Long awaited, he will never come in Europe
He will appear in Asia
One issued from the great Hermes
He will be over all the kings of the East

[*A great scientist-leader emerges from the
East*]